By Faith…

My Journey of Obedience

By Meagan Pinkney

By Faith: My Journey of Obedience

Copyright © 2020

Printed in the United States of America

ISBN: 978-0-9971852-4-9 (paperback)

ISBN: 978-0-9971852-5-6 (ebook)

Published by: Joseph's Ministry, LLC

www.josephsministryllc.com

Unless otherwise indicated all scriptural quotations are taken from the New Living Translation of the Bible.

All rights reserved. This book or any portion thereof may not be reproduced or used in any manner whatsoever without the express written permission of the publisher except for the use of brief quotations in a book review.

DEDICATION

This book is dedicated to every child of God needing encouragement along their Christian walk.

CONTENTS

Acknowledgments 1

Introduction 3

Chapter 1: Child's Play 5

Chapter 2: The Blessed Life 13

Chapter 3: The Ultimate Sacrifice 27

Chapter 4: Total Restoration 57

Principles To Live By 75

ACKNOWLEDGMENTS

I would first like to thank God the Father, God the Son, and God the Holy Spirit for choosing me to experience this amazing journey and sharing it with you! I would also like to acknowledge those individuals in my life—near and far—who have prayed for me and encouraged me and not judged me during my faith journey with Jesus.

Thank you!

INTRODUCTION

"Mama always said life is like a box of chocolates. You never know what you are going to get," stated Forrest Gump from the 1994 movie, Forrest Gump. These are exactly my thoughts as I continue to live my life for Christ. Two of my most popular phrases are, "I never thought my life would be this way," and "I wonder what is coming next?" Life is truly a blessing and is meant to be explored and enjoyed, but more importantly, a blessing. Are you willing to use your life for a greater purpose? I understand this is not the most popular thing to do in this age, but what if you allowed God to use your life in unorthodox ways to show the world His goodness, love, mercy, favor, and that He really does exist? "YES, of course," you may say! But are you willing to pay the cost to intimately pursue this lifestyle? In this book, I will share my powerful journey of obedience. Sharing real life examples of what it looks like to hear and obey the Holy Spirit, make mistakes, and do it all by faith. My testimony will surely bless your life and change your perspective of what it means to follow Christ…today.

God Bless

CHAPTER 1: CHILD'S PLAY

"When I was a child, I spoke and thought and reasoned as a child. But when I grew up, I put away childish things."
1 Corinthians 13:11

As a little girl, I really thought I was special. Yes, of course, every child probably thinks the same thing. But truly, I really did and still to this day think that I am special. Not special in my own eyes but in God's eyes. I can remember being prompted from within myself to read Psalms 23 every night before bed as a young child. In the process of time, I challenged myself to memorize the entire chapter and eventually I did. This prompting, from my recollection, was not created because of the Pastor's instructions to the congregation to read this particular passage nor was it the instructions from my parents. It was more. It was a deep and pure feeling from within myself.

I followed those instructions without a sure understanding of why this prompting was present and who sent it. As a result, the entire 23rd Psalm was the first passage of scripture that I had ever read on my own and memorized. My time in elementary school is my earliest memory of these inner promptings. Little did I know, it was God's Spirit leading and directing me. In retrospect, I had no idea what the Holy Spirit was shielding my family and me from because I was obeying His instruction, reading aloud, and memorizing His Word.

I can also remember times as a child when the Holy Spirit would have me to pray but specifically pray that He would use me. Not fully knowing what that meant, I would pray that prayer almost daily. Then I began to see a pattern. As I would pray, "Lord use me" the Lord would really use me, and from my various experiences of being used, I quickly correlated that to mean something "bad" was going to happen every time I would pray that. In my mind, something "bad" meant that I would have to go through something uncomfortable. As a result of my new found revelation, I stopped praying, "Lord use me" as if I was getting over on or out smarting God. As days or perhaps weeks went by, I would find myself praying once more, "Lord use me." And God being His faithful self, would do just that. You may be thinking, how can God use a child? I am glad that you asked! One example that stays fresh in my mind is from my third grade graduation. The ceremony was just about over when they began to introduce one final award, the citizenship award. I had no idea what that award stood for but soon I would find out. I remember the announcement going something like this, "And this award goes to Meagan Pinkney. Meagan, come receive your award." Looking around puzzled, I thought to myself, what?! I received the award, took pictures and smiled but I still did not know what the award was for. As the ceremony was dismissed and the students were escorted out of the cafeteria, some of my classmates asked me if they could *have* my award. I did not know what this award represented or what I did to receive it but I did know that it was mine and not theirs! I quickly asked my mom what the award was for and to my amazement, I learned that I received this citizenship award at my third grade graduation because I helped another third grader pass third grade! Me. Meagan Pinkney, an 8-year-old, helped another 8-year-old little girl get to the next level in our young education. How? That is a great question! I have NO idea! BUT I suspect that I was only being myself, Meagan Pinkney. It is true what they say; being you (good or bad) really does affect other people. According to my teachers, the person I helped was a good friend of mine. I probably noticed her not following instructions and corrected my friend in my unique 8-year-old way. I guess I corrected her enough times during the year that she developed a trust of my judgment and followed my lead. Whatever the case, several things transpired: (1) my friend passed third grade, (2) I cultivated my leadership skills, and (3) God used me. I was rewarded openly for something I did privately. Now that will preach! Are you encouraged yet?! Just keep reading…

As the years passed, these inner promptings (the Holy Spirit speaking to me) continued. God began using me in different ways. During my senior year of college, a good friend and I were talking on the phone one day and she was explaining that she was not going to have enough money to pay half of her rent for that particular month. During the conversation, I felt the Holy Spirit say, "pay the remaining balance." She never asked me for the money but why would she? We were both college students with not a whole lot of money, but I could not ignore the Holy Spirit. I told her I would pay her remaining balance and she was totally shocked. She said she would pay me back and she did. God used me! Those few examples may make my life sound easy—just hear and obey. Sike! Every time I have obeyed the voice of the Holy Spirit, it was all done BY FAITH. According to Hebrews 11:1, "Now faith is being sure of what we hope for and certain of what we do not see." I have learned from my experience that there is a fine line between stepping out on faith and being insane. The only difference is that faith is God inspired and insanity is not. I was a sophomore engineering student in college and it was time to begin exploring various companies for summer internships.

My two really good friends (one is a guy and the other a girl) and myself were embarking on this journey together. The guy friend secured his internship rather quickly with a great railroad company out of state. The girl friend and I were actually selected for an interview with the same company for the same position! It was with the Department of Transportation. We both interviewed on the same day, and we celebrated by stopping for burgers and tacos once the interviews were completed. I was totally confident that I would get the offer from that company, especially, over my friend for several reasons. My grade point average (GPA) was much higher than hers and I felt that I wanted that position more than she did. To my surprise, my friend was extended an offer and I was not! How could this happen?! My GPA was on point, I dressed nicely for the interview, I wanted the position, and I answered all the interview questions to the best of my ability. I did not understand! Do not get me wrong, I was really happy for my friend but I wanted to be happy for myself. Is that so wrong? Both of my friends had internships and I did not. Just great! When we returned to school after my friend had accepted the offer, it was like everyone in the engineering building knew that I did not get the position and several individuals asked about my plan. I honestly wanted to say, LEAVE ME ALONE, but I just smiled and said that I did not know yet. As the days went by, I vividly remember feeling lost, unaccomplished, embarrassed, and shameful—but a turning point in my life was on the horizon. Walking in the engineering building one day, the guy friend said to me, "Meagan, where is your faith?" What? Where is my faith? That is easy for him to say, he had an internship already secured and people were not asking him a million questions a day about what he was going to do! Whose side was my friend on, I thought to myself with a whooole lot of attitude. His words stung! Coming back to reality, I asked myself the same question. Meagan, where IS your faith? What am I doing? How did I get *here*? Did I even pray about this? On that day, I came to my senses and sought the Holy Spirit. HELP!

I interviewed with a couple of local engineering companies with a hope of getting an offer extended to me before the summer but no luck. I prayed a very specific prayer—that the Lord would send me my engineering internship before the summer started. I was currently working as a student worker for the State of Louisiana, so I had a job, but I desired an engineering job for the summer. Day after day, night after night I prayed my prayer. With absolutely no offers to consider, the more I prayed, the more I truly believed it would happen for me. I began to be genuinely happy and excited for the girl friend. We would talk on the phone and I would stay on her about getting everything they recommended that she needed to get to be prepared for the summer internship. My entire attitude changed as I decided to seek God regarding the matter and not lash out in anger towards my friends or anyone who would listen. I was in a place of rest and peace when something happened, suddenly! It was a Friday afternoon and I was at my student worker job when suddenly my cell phone rang. I looked at my phone but did not recognize the number. I thought about not answering it like I usually do but that day I was curious. I stepped outside the office into the hallway to have more privacy. "Hello." "Hello, may I speak to Meagan Pinkney?" "This is she."

"Great, Hi Meagan this is so and so from the Department of Transportation. Our committee has decided to extend the number of engineering interns we can accept this summer and I am calling to see if you are still interested?" "Wow, YES ma'am I am!" "Great, you start on Monday. Your direct manager will be expecting you." "Thank you so much." WOOOW! Look at God! My prayers were answered in the 11th hour. This happened on Friday and I started my summer engineering internship the first day of summer just as I prayed! There was NO way I could have predicted that I and the girl friend would be working for the same company after all! What a journey of faith! This situation was indeed the turning point of my faith journey. Thank you, Lord!

"Faith isn't a feeling. It's a choice to trust God even when the road ahead seems uncertain"
—*Dave Wil*

CHAPTER 2: THE BLESSED LIFE

"It is more blessed to give than to receive." Acts 20:35

"HAPPY NEW YEAR! 2014 is going to be a GREAT YEAR!" Yes, this is so, for most people but for me, it was the year that changed the trajectory of my ENTIRE life. If you have read my first book, Waiting While You Wait: My Journey Through Singleness, you know that my life is truly blessed to be a blessing. If you have not read this book yet, what are you waiting for?! The stories I can tell and the testimonies I can give from my journey are quite amazing. Not that I am amazing, but God and His power are amazing! For instance, in Waiting While You Wait I share about meeting the lady at the gas station:

After returning to Midland from my "business" trip to Tulsa for 3 months, a co-worker and I decided to catch up over lunch. We were eating at a restaurant, and I was telling her about my training in Tulsa. As we were wrapping up our lunch, the waitress came to give us our checks. Before I continue, I must say that my co-worker was Caucasian and her name could possibly pass for an African American lady's name in this day and age, however, I am an African American lady, and my name is Meagan. We both provided the waitress our credit cards with our checks. For some reason, the waitress decided to change our names. She handed me my co-worker's credit card with my check and handed my co-worker my credit card with her check! I was heated! In my mind, this was racial profiling! My co-worker paid me cash for the difference in our checks that was charged on my card because her meal was more expensive than mine. We left that place, never to return, and returned to work. This whole incident changed my mood for the rest of the day. I left work still a little upset and went to get some gas before arriving home not wanting to speak to anyone.

While pumping my gas, I heard someone say, "Ma'am, can you help me out?" I ignored the voice and continued pumping my gas. Seconds later, I heard the voice again, "Ma'am can you please help me out?" I started to look around, and the lady pumping her gas at the pump in front of me appeared to not hear this voice. I looked around my pump to find a middle aged Caucasian lady looking right at me, saying "Ma'am I forgot my wallet at home, and I do not have any money to buy my gas, can you please help me out?" I politely shrugged my shoulders as to say, "No, I cannot help you out." She pleaded with me as I thought to myself, what if that was me? What if I accidentally left my wallet at home and did not have any money to pay for my gas? Would anyone help me? I looked at the woman and said "Ma'am, let me finish pumping my gas and I will be over there in a second." I finished pumping my gas, locked my car, and walked over to her pump. She attempted to show me that she was really out of gas. In my head I thought, if you are lying, that is between you and God. I said "No need, I believe you." At this time, gas was around $2.00 plus for a gallon. My plan was to only put a gallon in her tank. But as I realized that she was driving a big suburban, a gallon was not going to get her out of the parking lot. While pumping her gas, she was telling me that she was really embarrassed. I filled up her tank with $10.00 worth of gas. I told her that I was finished and I put $10.00 in and she looked at me and started to cry! She ran to me and gave me a huge hug, cried some more, and gave me another big hug. She thanked me and I said, "No problem, just make it home safely." As I walked back to my car and turned around to see her, she was gone! She drove off so fast! I started my car and heard that still quiet voice say, that was an angel! WOW! This experience really opened my eyes and showed me that I must NEVER let my feelings, whether good or bad, get me so wound up and distracted because you never know when you will entertain angels. The enemy will bring traps into your life to get you to trip right before your blessing comes, but we must stay focused on waiting (serving) on God each and every day regardless of our feelings!

That same week of entertaining the angel of God, I obeyed the Holy Spirit and started the process of building my first house at the age of 24-years-old! To read more about this process and other testimonies check out my books, *Waiting While You Wait, Pray Eat Lift* and *Inner Circle*…you will certainly be encouraged.

In December 2013, I was relocated back to Tulsa, Oklahoma for work which means, from my experience with the Holy Spirit on this past 7-year journey that my assignment at my previous location was complete and a new assignment was on the horizon. But first things first, what church do I connect with? Well, this church finding process was a much quicker and different process from the others. Upon moving to Tulsa, I had enrolled in the Graduate degree program at

Oral Roberts University to obtain a Master's degree in Divinity. When I arrived in Tulsa in December 2013, my apartment was not quite ready so I stayed in a hotel for a couple of days and while there the Holy Spirit instructed me to find a new church home. I had lived in Tulsa previously but this move back was for a different assignment, therefore, I truly believed I was not to attend my previous church in Tulsa. Other than that church, I did not have any experience or knowledge of any other churches I could attend. Then suddenly the thought came to me to research churches connected with Oral Roberts University! That sounds like a really smart idea, right?! Yes, I thought so myself.

I searched online for a while then I came across a site for a church called Transformation Church. As I clicked on the site, I thought to myself that it was a strange name for a church. I navigated through the website and found the tab introducing the church's Pastors. I read the bios on each Pastor and spouse and surprisingly came across a familiar face! The church's worship leader visited my previous church in Houston for a worship night we were hosting. Sometime after the worship night, I transitioned from Houston to my next assignment and around the same time the worship leader (as they introduced was from New York) was transitioning to

Tulsa and Transformation Church where I would eventually call home! Coincidence? I think not! I quickly took this as a sign from Heaven and was right! BY FAITH!

From the start of the year, I was challenged by the Holy Spirit to give extravagantly to my church to help pay off the church building. I sowed around $20,000 on the first round and around $50,000 on the second round. Yes, these are LARGE amounts of money but notice my verbiage. I did not say I gave money to my church, I said I sowed into my church. For the record, I NEVER give money away. My money is seed and with planting seed it must always be planted (sown) into good ground to reap a bountiful harvest. It may sound crazy and unrealistic to some but the amount of money sown is not that important. What is important is the obedience attached to the sowing. I sowed those particular seeds into my church out of pure obedience to the Holy Spirit. Whether the Holy Spirit instructs you to give someone $5, obey God and sow $5 into that person's life. Several things occur when you obey God in these giving situations: 1. You never know if that person has been praying and asking God for the very thing the Holy Spirit just instructed you to give. Your obedience gives God the glory and increases that person's faith and trust in the Lord, and 2. I have been told several times, every time

God asks you to give something, He has your harvest in mind! Moral of this story—obey God!

After I had sown those two large seeds into my church in the first half of the year, I figured that my giving obligation was complete for the rest of the year. SIKE! At the time, I had NO IDEA what the Lord's plans were for my life. As time went on, the Holy Spirit continued to challenge or instruct me to sow at various times. I can remember being in a grocery store in the checkout line, minding my own business, when this middle aged African American couple walked up behind me in the line. Suddenly, I heard the still small voice prompt me to pay for their groceries. WHAT?! I turned around, not knowing who those people were. I smiled and glanced in their basket. They were only buying a gallon of vanilla Bluebell ice cream and a frozen apple pie. The wife, I assume, was pushing the basket and the husband was standing in front of the basket right behind me. When I turned around the first time, I saw the wife looking in her purse for her payment method but she looked very frustrated with the process. As I continued to stand in line for my turn to be checked out, I heard over and over again in my spirit to OBEY, OBEY, OBEY! Not knowing what else to do, I obeyed the Holy Spirit. The nice cashier finished checking me out and I purposefully (and nervously) took my time placing my receipt in my purse. While I was still near the machine to swipe my card, the cashier had already finished ringing up the couple's groceries behind me. I quickly slid my card to pay.

Then I gave the receipt to the couple and told them I took care of their groceries for them. The wife was still looking in her purse with no apparent luck. The husband smiled and said very peacefully, "that is what it is all about, God bless you." He told his wife what happened and she finally looked up and was relieved. I quickly walked to my car in awe of what God had done. To God be the glory!

Another amazing sowing time was in May 2014. I was attending and serving at the Gap Standers International Annual Prayer conference in Tulsa, OK and I attended one of their day sessions on this particular day. Towards the end of the ministering time, the speaker called a gentleman out of the crowd and began to prophesy to him, and the speaker instructed everyone to sow something into this man's life because God was about to bless him and his business. After all the sowing I had been doing, the human side of me was not necessarily excited about obeying the instructions. While the worship music played and praying in the spirit going on all around me, I closed my eyes to see if the Holy Spirit was actually instructing me, personally, to give at this time. I am not sure how long it was before I heard the Holy Spirit say, "Do you trust me?" I immediately burst into tears. Giving again?! I said, yes, I trust you and proceeded to grab my check book out of my purse. I wrote a check for $1,000 to sow it into that man's life and business. During that same weekend, I heard the Holy Spirit say that I would sow every dime in my savings account before the end of the conference. I did not respond nor acknowledge what I heard because surely I had to be TRIPPING! The next night at the conference, I heard it again. REALLY! Okay, okay…I hear you, Lord. Think I am crazy yet? Out of my mind? Looney?

Well, I have learned during my walk with the Lord that there is a fine line between being out of your mind and walking by faith. Praise God that my experience and testimonies prove that I am walking by faith. So, back to the conference. Each offering opportunity after I finally realized that the Holy Spirit was instructing me to give once more, I gave a specific amount that would ensure that my savings account would read $0 by the end of the conference. Now, you are probably wondering how much money I had in the savings account in question. I had a little over $6,000 in that particular account. I sowed all $6,000 into that conference and ministry with peace. I had assurance that I heard from the Lord and He always knows what He is doing. Surely He knows, right? Well, to ease any last minute doubts I had, another guest in the conference took the mic one night because she wanted to share what the Lord had instructed her to do during the conference. She introduced herself and began to tell the crowd that the Holy Spirit instructed her to...guess? Yep, sow every dime she had from one of her accounts! No way! Her testimony gave me soooo much peace. I was not the only one the Holy Spirit was challenging to give at this level. At the end of the conference, every dime I had in that savings account was sown! Wow! What a feeling of expectation of what the Lord was going to do. I just had to speak with the lady who spoke up at the conference. During my conversation with her, I knew I did the right thing. Also, she prayed for me, prophetically. She began to say that in 30 days the Lord would give me more money than I sowed. HALLELUJAH! I received that Word from God! I had no idea of the journey of faith I was entering.

Another testimony I can recall is during my process of writing my first book. Honestly, I never really wanted to write a book in my life. One day, I felt in my spirit to start journaling the journey I was on with the Lord as well as all the amazing things I had experienced, learned, and witnessed. Initially, I thought my journaling was to be used as a little book just for my family and children to come to read about my life. It could be an encouragement to them and point them to the Lord. I lived in Houston, Texas when this journaling assignment came to me. While in Houston, I met a dear friend of mine who was getting ready to release her first book from her own book publishing company. As time went on, I moved from Houston, back to Louisiana and then back to Tulsa. I remember this Houston friend texting me one morning before work asking for prayer of agreement as the Lord had instructed her to go on her first book tour, but she was nervous and did not have a lot of money to do so. Of course, I agreed with her in prayer regarding her request. On my way to work that same morning, while praying for her, the Holy Spirit really choked me up regarding her request. What is it? While I was praying to Him to supply my friend's need, the Holy Spirit was instructing me to sow a seed into her book tour. Wow. Okay Lord! I was instructed to sow $1,000 into her tour. I did not tarry. I obtained the money order and mailed the seed to my friend as soon as possible. She was totally shocked (as was but we both gave God all the glory and praise! Little did I know how this seed would be manifested into my life. My friend's book was released and she went on to have a great book tour at various military bases in the United States!

Meanwhile, in Tulsa, I continued my journaling process. As time went on, I would meet people in various places and felt led to share a piece of my testimony to encourage them along their walk. Well…my sharing time with these people was increasing and I found myself not having enough time to really share the meat of my testimony but each person I encountered encouraged me to write my testimony in a book. I completely blew the "write a book" idea away. Not realizing the Holy Spirit was constantly speaking to me through these people and setting me up. Finally, one day I woke up and said to myself, "I am going to write a book!" It was settled within me and it was time. But how do I write and publish a book? I am not famous nor do I know anyone that has written a book. Before discouragement could set in, I remembered my friend from Houston that had just written and self-published her first book! Only God could make those Kingdom connections. I love it! I contacted her about possibly publishing my first book and she agreed. But wait, there is more! She not only agreed to publish my first book but remember that seed I sowed into her book tour some time ago? Well, the harvest had manifested! Because of my obedience in sowing that seed for her book tour, she blessed me with her publishing services for my book! To be clear, my publishing services was PAID IN FULL! My seed went before me and opened doors that only God could do. I had NO IDEA what that seed was for when I sowed it but God had my harvest in mind the entire time! Hallelujah! One seed after the other. One faith step after the other.

As you can tell from my testimonies in this chapter, living the blessed life is not what you think. Initially, I thought living the blessed life meant I lived a life with a lot of great stuff just for myself (i.e., mansion, fine cars, fine clothes, money...etc.). But the Holy Spirit has shown me that living the blessed life is just the opposite. Do not believe me? The scripture says in Acts 20:35, 'It is more blessed to give than to receive.' Having possession of these great things is only half of the story. Having the heart and ability to release possession of these great things when prompted by the Holy Spirit is the true blessed life!

"When you focus on being a blessing, God makes sure that you are always blessed in abundance."
-Joel Osteen

FAITH BREAK

¹⁷ It was by faith that Abraham offered Isaac as a sacrifice when God was testing him. Abraham, who had received God's promises, was ready to sacrifice his only son, Isaac, ¹⁸ even though God had told him, "Isaac is the son through whom your descendants will be counted." ¹⁹ Abraham reasoned that if Isaac died, God was able to bring him back to life again. And in a sense, Abraham did receive his son back from the dead.

Hebrews 11:17-19 New Living Translation (NLT)

CHAPTER 3: THE ULTIMATE SACRIFICE

"Obedience is better than sacrifice." 1 Samuel 15:22

It is now 2015 and I am expecting great things this year. Frankly, after all the sowing of finances in 2014 I am expecting to reap a harvest out of this world! Do you remember the prophecy I received from the lady at the conference? She said after my sowing and obeying the Holy Spirit at the conference that I would receive more money than I sowed. Well, it came to pass around the exact time she mentioned. Soon after this experience, I had an opportunity to go to another level with my giving to advance the Kingdom of God in new ways— investments. This team of investors presented to me and others some projects they were working on in their city. They were looking for other Kingdom minded people to partner with them on future projects. After much, much prayer I decided to move forward with the investments that promised to help God's people and I would be blessed financially in the process. I did not receive any warning signs or checks in my spirit regarding moving forward so BY FAITH it was. Taking instructions from the team of investors a larger amount of money was received, and everything was going great!

Bring it on 2015, bring it on! Every year my church, like most churches, start the New Year off with a fast. For the first 21 days of the year, we prayed and fasted for direction and clarity for the new year. My fast started off great! I began to feel God's presence like never before. The Holy Spirit started telling me how much He loved me and the great plans He had in store for my purpose. I absolutely loved my quiet time with the Holy Spirit. God is such a good Father! Regardless of the troubles we may face, God is still on the Throne of Heaven. He is willing and able to move and work on our behalf…if we let Him. He loves when we call upon His name—Abba Father, the Great I AM, the Great Counselor, Prince of Peace, Friend, Provider and the list goes on! One day, during our corporate time of prayer at my church, the Holy Spirit instructed me to go on a book tour for my first book that I planned to release March 2015. A book tour? That is interesting. I journaled this instruction and wondered how this would work out. On the very last day of our 21 day fast, the Holy Spirit brought to my attention another matter that had been in my spirit, but I did not pursue nor inquire from the Holy Spirit the meaning. The Holy Spirit was presenting me with an opportunity to walk BY FAITH. Yes, these opportunities do come to God's children quite often, but most times we ignore it or quickly dismiss the thought because it is not a convenient time for us. Frankly, these opportunities come so that God can use us to show His power in the Earth. 2 Chronicles 16:9 (NKJV) says, "For the eyes of the Lord run to and fro throughout the whole earth, to show Himself strong on behalf of those whose heart is loyal to Him." A thought to ponder: is your heart loyal to God? I thank God greatly for not allowing this faith opportunity to pass me by. And I thank God for this 21 day fast because my spirit man became ultra sensitive to the things of the spirit. Well…Meagan, get to the point, what was this grand faith opportunity? The Holy Spirit gave me the option to quit my engineering job and work in full-time ministry (pursuing Him)! Now, let's evaluate the conditions of my life at this moment. I am a single woman, no children, not a whole lot of savings (thanks to my obedience in 2014 to sow on another level), making nearly 6 figures with nothing holding me back. Again, I thank God for fasting because I had supernatural peace about this opportunity. I did not know what this full-time ministry aspect looked like because I technically was not in ministry. I quit my job to obey Jesus! Everything was strangely coming together. I began to plan my last days at my job—which month to leave. As those thoughts overwhelmed me I had the strangest feeling in my spirit that I did not have a lot of time to make my move. It was either now or never—no pressure! Reader, please hear me, I did not WANT to quit my job. I really liked my job, but these faith opportunities also come to test us and show what is really in your heart. Would I trust my job or God to provide my daily needs? We would soon find out but I was definitely stepping out BY FAITH. At this point of my faith journey, this was indeed the ultimate sacrifice. Would you sacrifice it all for God's glory? He sacrificed His only son for us! According to the Merriam-Webster dictionary, the word sacrifice means an act of offering to a deity (God) something precious or the surrender of something for the sake of something else. I was surrendering my job (by faith) for the sake of knowing and trusting God on another level. I do not believe the Holy Spirit would have placed this opportunity in my spirit if I did not have the faith capacity to carry this through. This was not a decision I made from my own being because I felt it was time for another level in God. Therefore, I am not encouraging anyone to just quit their jobs to follow Jesus….unless you believe He is calling you out. God gives us His grace when we choose to obey Him and step out BY FAITH.

The last day of the fast was on a Sunday and I knew on Monday morning at work I needed to figure out when my two weeks would start. That Sunday night, I decided to continue my fasting and seek wise counsel and prayer on this matter. After I had received my confirmation, I was assured that this was the Holy Spirit leading me and my decision was to walk BY FAITH. Monday morning comes and I did not say a word to anyone about my decision to leave the company. The entire work day I honestly tried to talk myself out of this decision. But every time I tried the Holy Spirit would bring back to my mind something my Pastor said during one of his recent sermons. One of the wisdom nuggets was that "God does not call us out to be comfortable." All day—from 8am to 4pm—I went back and forward in my mind about really stepping out BY FAITH and leaving my job. By 4:30pm, I said my last prayer regarding this matter and gave it all to God. I submitted my two-week notice via email to my manager and not even 30 seconds later my manager called me on my work phone. I briefly explained the situation and had peace about my decision. The next day my manager submitted my notice to HR and said she is trying to get me a severance package but that did not work out. I was a little upset but quickly realized that if I had received a severance package, I would have had to leave the premises immediately. There was a reason I needed these two weeks at the job.

During my last two weeks, I had the amazing opportunity to share this faith opportunity with several of my coworkers who were Christians. From their comments to me, they were really encouraged in their faith in God because of my decision to walk BY FAITH. One co-worker came to my cubicle and said that the Holy Spirit had been dealing with her about stepping out BY FAITH on some things. I told her what the Holy Spirit told me, "If I take care of His business, He would take care of mine." This was based on the scripture Matthew 6:33 that says, "But seek first his kingdom and his righteousness, and all these things will be given to you as well." I also remember leaving work one day during the two weeks, and I heard the Holy Spirit say, "guess what they are talking about in there (the office)?" I said, "I do not know." He said, "Me." Well, praise the Lord! That is what He really wants. God wants His name to be glorified in the Earth! This was really comforting to me because I was being really intentional about making sure people understood this step of faith had absolutely nothing to do with me but everything to do with what God was doing at this time. On my last day at work, they threw me a party and gave me gifts! This was all great but what really took the cake was that on my last day at work, I received an invitation to be one of the speakers at an upcoming Woman's conference in town! That was nothing but God reassuring me yet again that He was in this.

I do not want to just hurry through telling you about one of the biggest decisions of my life, therefore, I want to provide you with a recap. I was fasting and seeking God for 21 days for clarity and direction for my life in this season. The last day of the fast, the Holy Spirit instructed me clearly to quit my great engineering job and follow Him. Out of obedience and truly BY FAITH, I quit my great engineering job to follow Jesus somewhere unknown to me. I had very little cash in my savings account but a great amount of peace in my spirit. I was ridiculed by some and cheered on by a few but God was with me through it all. I really want to stress the fact that I was fasting for 21 days! Fasting is a sacrifice, but this sacrifice does wonders to your spirit man and also KILLS your flesh! If I had not been fasting, there would be no testimony of

Meagan Pinkney quitting her great engineering job to follow Jesus. Are you crazy?! No ma'am and no sir. The fact that I really quit, obeying Jesus, is a testament of the power of fasting! Therefore, I am the first to say that my life is not perfect but God's power and plan for His children is and obeying Him is wise.

After I had quit my job, things were relatively normal for me for a while. My devotion time with the Lord was extended, my workout schedule remained but I rested a lot! I began reading more spiritual books and seeking God for my next steps but no immediate answers were provided. I felt the need to intentionally take this time to rest for the journey ahead. Although I remained in my apartment and carried on, as usual, the first day after leaving my job I thought to myself, I am canceling my alarm system, cable, internet…etc. to save money. But I was immediately checked by the Holy Spirit. One thing that the Holy Spirit dealt with me about was not having a poverty mindset. I was and will never be poor! But if I would have shut all those services off because I was looking in the natural and looking at my bank account, I would have birthed that spirit into my mind, and eventually, it would have manifested in my environment. Instead, I chose to trust God and His plan for my life. I intentionally sought out scriptures that I could stand on during this time. One scripture being Philippians 4:19 which says, "And this same God who takes care of me will supply all your needs from his glorious riches, which have been given to us in Christ Jesus." I have held this scripture and many others in a choke hold. I was building my own faith in God's word but also reminding God of His word and promises to me. As this transition was taking place from my job, another transition was taking place into ministry just as the Lord stated during the fast.

A few months prior I became a new team member of a traveling international evangelism ministry based out of Tulsa called Gap Standers International. When the instructions came to me to quit my job, I agreed to obey but presented my desires to the Lord at the same time. I told the Holy Spirit that I wanted to travel during this time, work for Him by helping the Kingdom of God advance in the Earth, and not have to ever be concerned about money. All of these desires and more were fulfilled during this journey of following and trusting Jesus. Soon after I quit my job, I was nominated (initially without me knowing) to be the ministry assistant for Gap Standers due to the current assistant feeling the need to step down. This was a sudden transition, but I felt was timely. During my serving God through Gap Standers International,

I was able to travel full time with the ministry to various states and cities I had never been, get exposed to how it feels to be in full time traveling ministry, coordinator for their annual prayer conference, administrator of various aspects of the business side of the ministry and travel to South Africa! So many great things were happening in 2015 already! I quit my job in February 2015, my first book was released in March 2015, I ministered at my first women's conference in May 2015, went on my first book tour June 2015, and traveled to South Africa for two weeks in August 2015! While in South Africa, I had an opportunity to speak to students at a high school and encourage them in their studies. I also had the opportunity to sell my recently released book, personally, internationally! What a time, what a time! My dreams were coming true. I was having the time of my life. I was now getting used to my flexible schedule and full-time ministry lifestyle. It is like my life started once I quit my job. However, I did miss the engineering paychecks every two weeks. I paid my apartment's rent, cable and internet, alarm system, and electric bill every month as if I was working a full-time job. It was and is still imperative to trust God to provide no matter what the situation. I did not come this far in my life by not trusting Him, but this trusting was on an entirely different level. It removed all pride (known and unknown) from my life. Who was I now? No job, practically no money coming in, no professional status. Nothing. It appeared that I had nothing to the world but I have everything because I have God on my side. I have sacrificed my "worth" to follow Jesus. You think I am strange? Never heard of Jesus asking anyone to leave their jobs before to follow Him? It is actually quite common. Look at the lives of the twelve disciples. One by one Jesus asked them to leave their way of life, their way of making ends meet to follow Him. And they did! They trusted Him and followed Jesus and while on this journey with Jesus all of their needs were met. This was my hope and confidence. Not fully knowing where this journey was taking me, my WHY for saying yes to the Lord was sure. Plus, I was too far into this journey and walk with Him to turn back now! I wanted to see what the end was going to be.

Once I returned from South Africa, I felt a shift on the horizon. Before I left on this mission's trip, I felt in my spirit that I would be moving to Dallas, Texas. This was confirmed after my trip from Africa. It was also revealed to me after I returned from Africa that God was sending me back to engineering! As you could imagine, I was completely taken aback. I thought I "retired" from engineering work and corporate America for good but I guess not. First, the news of me moving to Dallas. Now this! On the edge of your seat yet? Moving was definitely not in my plan during this phase of my life. I was used to relocating with the company I was working for. They packed my things and delivered them safe and sound to my new place. But this move was different. There was no company moving me and I surely did not have the extra money lying around for moving purposes. Regardless of my thoughts, the Holy Spirit informed me that I was about to move. I thank God for the Holy Spirit because He really does lead and guide us in the way we should go.

But before any move could take place, my next divine assignment was to officially start my non-profit. In my second book, I introduced my non-profit called the Joseph Foundation, and its purpose to provide clothes and nonperishable food items to those less fortunate. I even started this foundation by faith being directed by the Holy Spirit. Earlier in the year, I began spreading the word about my efforts of obtaining gently used clothes from family and friends around town. I already had a climate controlled storage unit not far from my apartment with several things I had acquired along the way. Mainly furniture and appliances from when I had my house in Texas. The clothes I obtained for the foundation was placed in my personal storage with really no plans of getting a second storage designated for the foundation due to the money commitment for the second storage. I was reminded, "if we want God to laugh just tell Him your plans." One day I stopped by my storage unit to pay my payment for the month when as I was driving away I heard the Holy Spirit speaking. He instructed me to go back into the storage unit office and ask about the smallest storage they had available to be used for the foundation. Thinking to myself, another bill?!? BUT I desire to fully obey God. I have learned that obedience is a learned behavior and obedience keeps you protected. So I quickly turned my car around and headed back to the storage office. There was a 5 x5 storage available for $50/month. Me being me, I kindly asked if they had any discounts available. The worker replied, "no, only student discounts." Wait, what!? I am currently a student at Oral Roberts University, can I use this discount for this storage and for my other storage? "Yes, of course, she replied!" Really?! I left there with my new foundation's storage and a discount on my personal storage and the foundation's storage! Praise God! While I was completing the paperwork for the new storage, the worker asked me about the purpose of the storage. I explained my newly formed foundation and my collection efforts. She was impressed and asked if she also could donate to my foundation! She ended up donating two bags of clothes! My God is good! Immediately, my collection of donated clothes picked up quickly but not before my capacity to handle the increase expanded. Before I stepped out by faith to get this second storage for the foundation only, I had only collected a few small bags of clothes. After the storage was obtained, it feels like the increase happened overnight! Shortly after that, I turned in the 5x5 storage for the foundation and expanded to a 10x10 storage full of clothes for the foundation! After my Africa trip, The Joseph Foundation was fresh on my mind. My thoughts were to plan for the foundation's first donation giveaway. I must note, the foundation received tons of clothes for donation without any advertising from myself. It was mainly word of mouth and, of course, the hand of the Lord moving. It was around October 2015 and it was recommended to me to host an event near or around the Thanksgiving holiday. Shortly afterwards, I heard about a free event being hosted by another local organization for the North Tulsa community and I had the opportunity to host my donation giveaway event in conjunction with this event! It was a great success. The organization was able to bless so many families in need of clothes and shoes in the

North Tulsa community. One family had just moved to Tulsa with nothing and was staying in a hotel in town. The mother and her children were blessed with more than enough. After the event was over, the foundation still had several bags of clothes and shoes, therefore, we were able to bless other local organizations that provided clothes to the homeless and incarcerated. What a blessing! My vision is to have distribution centers all over the World!

Now since the donation event was completed, I had the time to really focus on what the Holy Spirit was saying regarding the move to Dallas. One quiet day in my apartment, I heard the Holy Spirit tell me to sell all of my things in my personal storage. I was on my way to dismiss what I felt but figured why not walk by faith?! This could be an opportunity for God to show Himself strong in the Earth through me. What the heck. I will do it…BY FAITH of course! After I had received the instructions, I began to make mental notes regarding the selling price of my things. That night I texted a friend of mine in town about me selling my things. She asked me how much was I selling my washer and dryer for. I started to text her back with the price I had predetermined, but in my spirit, I felt not to release the price but tell her I would inform her about the price the following day. During the night the

Holy Spirit asked me to sow the washer and dryer into my friend who asked me for the price. I totally forgot that she needed a washer and dryer set but the Lord did not forget. The next day at church I found my friend and told her what the Holy Spirit instructed me to do—sow the washer and dryer set into her life. She was sooo surprised and ecstatic! After she had calmed down, she said something that made me surprised and ecstatic. The night before when I told her about me selling my things in the storage, she prayed and asked God to speak to my heart and ask me to sow the washer and dryer into her life! Really?!? Wow…I had no idea! I was just obeying what the Holy Spirit was telling me. That really encouraged me on so many levels. I never want my testimonies to seem as if walking by faith is a cake walk. Absolutely not, however, the Word of God says, "It is through faith that a righteous person has life." (Romans 1:17). These little confirming things that God provides give me peace that I am hearing His voice through the Holy Spirit and that I am heading in the right direction. It is all for His glory anyway! As days passed, the Holy Spirit showed me a way to sell my things quickly. I found a group on Facebook that was local to Tulsa to display the items. Not familiar with the process, I began to follow the other posts. I took pictures of my things and posted with the prices. Not everything was sold but the Holy Spirit instructed me to sow some things into people's lives. With over several thousand people connected to this group on Facebook, 95% of the individuals that purchased my things were people from my church! This gave me comfort because I had to meet the buyers and attending church with a majority of the people made me feel safer. The other 5% were people I had never met or seen in my life. I had interesting encounters with two different ladies. The first lady, from our communication prior, informed me that she was in school and would meet me after taking an exam. When we met, naturally, I asked her how her exam went. She really appreciated that. Another lady I met told me she looked up my personal Facebook page and saw I was a Christian then asked me if I could pray for her grandchild and her health. That is nobody but God! And yes, I did pray for them.

I ended up selling or sowing everything from my personal storage in record timing! One day after arriving home, I stopped in the living room and looked around at the things in my apartment and asked a single question to God, "What about these things?" Needless to say, I sold/sowed all the furniture in my apartment and only kept the personal items that could fit in my Honda Accord. One thing I must mention, the timing of these events were parallel to me receiving a letter from my apartment leasing office about my 1-year lease coming to an end in December. At the time, it was around Octoberish and they needed a 30-day notice on whether I would stay or move out. I did not know what to do. On the one hand, the Holy Spirit was telling me I would be moving to Dallas and has instructed me to sell all my things. On the other hand, my apartment lease was ending in a few months, and I had nowhere to go (with no stuff). I contacted my leasing office and asked for an extension on the 30-day notice requirement. It was approved, thankfully! Now what? Let us pray! I prayed and several thoughts came to me. 1. Am I walking BY FAITH if I sign another lease on my apartment while continuing to pray and believe God to send the money for rent? 2. Am I walking BY FAITH if I do not sign the lease and move from Tulsa? However, I remembered, every year for Christmas I travel back to Louisiana to spend time with my family and friends. Maybe, just maybe, I could head to Louisiana for Christmas and surely by the first of the year, God would have opened up the door for me to move to Dallas, right? After much prayer and meditating on 2 Chronicles 16:9, I felt the Holy Spirit leading me to not renew my lease and head to Louisiana for Christmas. I had a plan! It was early December and everything I had previously owned was gone! One thing I truly felt the Holy Spirit saying in my quiet time during this part of the journey was that I needed to travel light for where I was going. Where am I going, I thought to myself? Close to my time of departure from Tulsa, I was invited to attend a church service with a friend. Not knowing much about the church I attended believing that the Holy Spirit was leading me there for a particular reason, therefore, I was not leaving without getting what was mine. The service was great and I entered the prayer line after service for the Pastor to agree with me in prayer regarding me moving. I purposefully did not go into details with my prayer request but simply mentioned that I was moving. I left church that night receiving so much clarity and confirmation from the Holy Spirit regarding this shift in my life. I received more peace in my spirit! It was now time—a friend and her daughter came over to my apartment to help me with the final cleaning and bye, bye Tulsa! I traveled to Louisiana for the holidays not mentioning a word to my family about me moving.

After being home (Louisiana) for a few days, my mom came to me and inquired about all that stuff being packed in my car. I gently stated, well, I am moving to Dallas. She asked, "when?" I told her that I did not know. "The Holy Spirit told me I was moving." Expectedly, my mom said, "Ok Meagan and just walked away." Needless to say, leaving my job 10 months prior was a tough pill to swallow for my family. Probably thinking I had totally lost my mind, I could not give any energy to anything but spending time with the Holy Spirit and seeking direction from Him. If others were uncomfortable with my life at this point, how do you think I was feeling? I was NOT comfortable for one second, however, the peace of God was inside of me.

Christmas came and went, yet still no sign of an open door to Dallas. Early January came and I was invited to assist at a women's ministry event in Dallas. I was really not interested in attending the event. I just wanted to know my next step. However, I got over myself and traveled to Dallas for a few days. While serving at the conference, I greeted one of the speakers and business woman there. She began to express her need for an Operations Manager for her consulting company located in Dallas! Then to my surprise she said, "I hear you are moving to Dallas. Is that correct?" Hmmm? I told her yes. "Great," she replied. "Call me on Monday if you are interested in this opportunity." Wow…Great! But before you get excited, I just had to tell her my situation. I looked her in her eyes to tell her what was going on. I said I was interested in learning more about the position. I am moving to Dallas but I do not have a place to stay. She smiled and said, "Call me on Monday and do not worry about that." This business woman ended up calling me on Sunday to give me additional information and to learn of my experience and background. It would take an additional two months before I moved to Dallas as the Holy Spirit instructed me. I surely did not expect it to take three months total for my transition from Tulsa to Dallas by way of Louisiana. But I did have the opportunity to spend some quality time with my family and friends back home. While home, I had the honor of helping to plan and execute my mom's 60th birthday party which turned out great! This time home was not all bad, right? Well, with all the joy of being home, let's not forget my faith walk which being home all day was a consistent reminder of my journey. It was not easy for me. Being someone who prides herself in handling her business, in the natural, I appeared to be like a lost dog. No job, little money, no stuff (only my clothes), no home of my own, not stable BUT God was on my side all along. People tried to figure me out, make excuses for me and my actions (to others), but I was sticking strong to my conviction and promises from God. When I least expected it or needed the encouragement, the Holy Spirit would have friends contact me and sow seeds (money) into my life! Some friends knew the situation and some friends did not know any details at all. All smiles, I just thanked God! He is so faithful and is pleased with those who walk BY FAITH. It was imperative that I stayed in His presence and rehearsed His many promises to me—if not this walking on water experience would quickly turn into a swim for safety episode.

I was waiting for the day to transition to Dallas, in the meantime, I decided to actively apply for engineering positions in the Dallas/Ft Worth area. I must say, I have never received so many rejection notices in my life for positions I have applied for! At first, it was funny, but after a while, I began to get discouraged. Therefore, I took a break from my job searching. The day finally came for me to transition to Dallas and I was ready! Ready for what? I had no idea. The business woman invited me to stay at her home while I was working for her. No big deal but I was really out of my comfort zone to another degree! But if this is God, I am good. God does everything in His perfect timing and it is our responsibility to move when we see Him moving. The day after I arrived in Dallas, I heard that the Louisiana-Texas border was closed due to the main interstate being flooded!

Wow, perfect timing. The next phase of this journey has officially started. It was now entering April 2016. After being in Dallas a short time, I was presented with the opportunity to travel to various military bases in the United States to present and sell my books. Military bases book tour? Wait, where have I heard this before? YES, my friend, the author, and publisher of my first book! Remember, that seed I sowed into her first book tour—she went around to various military bases selling her book! Wow, this sowing and reaping principle is pretty serious! LESSON: Everything that you sow you will reap. I am not just speaking about money but everything. In Galatians 6:7, His Word states, "Do not be deceived, God is not mocked; for whatever a man sows, this he will also reap." This is a life principle for believers and non-believers. I sowed specifically into her book and book tour, and I have reaped a publishing deal that I was blessed with and connections to have a book tour at military bases that I was blessed with. My seeds were sown into fertile ground and went before me, and now it is harvest time for that seed!

I decided to call my book tour the Freedom book tour and started right after the Easter Holiday. I was extremely nervous about this military experience. 1. I had never been on a base/post. 2. I did not consider myself a sells person. 3. I would be at each base/post for one full week. Let us pray! Being prepped for this experience, I was informed of the atmosphere and was also advised to create additional merchandise. I already had two books, so I created t-shirts to go with each book. Now I am set! I headed back to Louisiana for my first scheduled location. I set up my products at the kiosks assigned and expected a great day. Starting my day at 8am, I asked the Holy Spirit to help me and give me the courage to stop these individuals and that my books would really encourage them. It was now or never—I stopped the first person that passed by my booth. "Hey, do you like to read?" I asked. "No," he replied as he kept walking. Okay. I thought to myself, this is really going to help me get over any rejection issues that I had—just great. Pulling myself together, I stopped the next person. "Hello, do you like to read?" I asked. "No thanks," he replied as he kept walking. Okay. I know it is early but really?! When I was being prepped, I was encouraged to start my conversations by saying, "hello, do you like to read?" Obviously, that was not working for me as it worked for the person that prepped me. It reminded me of the time when King Saul gave David his very own armor to wear to go fight against Goliath. After taking a few steps, David quickly realized it would be best that he took another man's armor off and be himself. With that being said, let me put another person's introduction down and be myself. Like David, I had to encourage myself, pray and watch God move! I stopped the next person and began to really be myself and introduce my products for sale. This guy was really nice and stopped and listened to my speech but did not have the money to purchase anything. I thanked him and awaited my next customer. Not even 5 minutes later, that same guy I just spoke with who did not have enough money came back and gave me a few dollars because he wanted to support me. Wow! Really? Thank you, Lord! I was really grateful and that was my first profit of the day. After a few times stopping and speaking to individuals, I was getting more and more comfortable. The first day, I sold around 11 items! That is great for my first time. I was drained after the first day and realized I was on a military base. Now, you may be thinking, Meagan did you not realize that when you first arrived. Yes and no. I was a little overwhelmed about this entire situation. This was indeed a new experience for me. But it never really hit me that these are the very people that are trained to go fight for our country. What am I doing here!? These people go through a lot for the sake of protecting our country. When I realized that, I began to take my sole focus from selling books to praying for these men and women. This is ministry! I do not believe being there was an accident. I believed and prayed that my testimonies in my books would be such an encouragement and light to all the readers at this base/post. The next day, I sold around 30 books and the numbers were consistent throughout the week! That is great news but the greater news was the people I had the honor to meet and encourage in the Lord. I even prayed with some at my booth. During this same week, I also received two invites to different churches in the area to sell my products, speak, and encourage their congregation after their bible study period. Wow! This was nobody but God! This week was full and productive. I was able to get over my fear of approaching people and getting out of my comfort zone. Many of the people that I stopped just gave me a donation to support my ministry and gave me hugs to encourage me along the way. The really encouraging part was when the soldiers purchased my books one day and a day or two later they would come back to ask me questions about the Lord, my journey, and they felt comfortable enough to share their journey with me. I believe they were blessed but I know I left that base as the blessed one. As I made my way back to Dallas, I began to reflect on my week and realize that God really set me up. This military base book tour had very little to do with me just selling books and leaving. But had everything to do with me walking through the open doors that He set open for me to introduce Him to others in a new way—my books—my testimony. What an honor! Had I not obeyed and even wrote these books, these doors would have never been opened. Think about your own life, what are just a few things that you believe the Holy Spirit has to do that would help so many people, but you had not started yet? Or you are waiting for the right time? The time is now! People need what you have to offer.

Over the next two months, I traveled to other military bases and my experience was unique at each base but my assignment was still the same. God is so good! Things were going well for me. I had just booked another military base, and while looking at my schedule to make additional bookings, the Holy Spirit put a block in my spirit. I truly felt to stop and not make any additional bookings at military bases. What?! This was my primary source of income, Lord. Nevertheless, I obeyed the instructions and wondered what the Lord was cooking up now. I told the business woman about what the Holy Spirit told me, and she got excited. She told me that means that the Lord was about to open another stream of income for me. Hallelujah!

A week before I was scheduled to be at my next and last military base, I received a call from someone in Tulsa wondering when I was coming back to visit because someone needed assistance with starting their nonprofit organization. I put in my schedule to travel to Tulsa after I completed my week at the military base. It was also perfect timing because I was still assisting the ministry in Tulsa and their annual conference was coming up. I wanted to be there to support them as well. During my devotion time one day, the Holy Spirit instructed me to pack up and bring all the things I brought with me to Dallas. I did not even think to question why but I just obeyed His instructions. However, not fully knowing His plans I did not share this with the business woman. I waited until everyone left the house and packed up my car.

What a journey! But I believe this is just the beginning. Our lives as followers of Christ should be full of abundant life and adventure. Every day is a new day for me, but I give all the glory, honor and praise to the one, true and living God!

"Obedience to God is the pathway to the life you really want to live."

–Joyce Meyer

CHAPTER 4: TOTAL RESTORATION

"I will give you back what you lost to the swarming locusts, the hopping locusts, the stripping locusts, and the cutting locusts"

Joel 2:25

I had just arrived in Wichita Falls, Texas at my last military post stop for my book tour. God has blessed me with great success during this book tour to various military and Air Force posts. Therefore, I expected nothing less with this trip. My first day at the post was great but the days to follow were getting slower and slower. This was a smaller post and the volume of people coming in the exchange was minimal. After praying about it, I made an executive decision to leave this post much sooner than my normal seven days. I did not feel the need to continue to rack up hotel nightly charges and not be making any money. I made a phone call to my friends in Tulsa and informed them of my sooner than expected arrival.

On the road again, but this time with all of my personal items packed in my car. Once I arrived in Tulsa, I tried contacting the woman I headed to Tulsa to meet with regarding her non-profit—no answer. Not a problem, I could just spend some time catching up with some friends and enjoying my visit. I tried calling the woman again the next day and the next—still no answer. Really?! It was Sunday and I was excited about going back to my church for fellowship. It is always an awesome time but this particular Sunday I received some instructions. The night before the Holy Spirit instructed me to contact the current leader of the prayer ministry and ask if it was okay if I join them for Sunday morning prayer in the prayer room. She totally agreed. During our prayer session, I met a woman of God who I had never met before. Coincidently, we ended up sitting next to each other during the church service. At some point during the service, she smiled at me then leaned over to let me know she would like to speak with me after service. I had never met her before, but I felt in my spirit this talk would be a right on time talk. And it was! The Holy Spirit used her to bring another level of peace to my spirit and to confirm my move back to Tulsa after being away for only 6 months. Wow, how quickly things can shift when you are walking BY FAITH and God is truly leading you. I informed the business woman that I was not returning, but if she needed any assistance from me, we could possibly work something out. My life has changed again but now I am back in Tulsa. I guess the third time is the charm. Now that I was sure to be moving back, where would I live? My location was changing again and my income from the book tour ceased, but God! The pastors from the ministry I was still assisting in Tulsa had invited me to stay at their home. Praise God for favor! God will never send you somewhere without providing along the way. During this entire faith walk with the Lord, I have not failed to receive everything I needed to survive. Jesus says in Luke 22:35 (NKJV), "When I sent you without money bag, knapsack, and sandals, did you lack anything? So they said, "Nothing." I have lacked nothing since the Lord has sent me off on this journey! God is always faithful to perform His word.

In the midst of all this excitement, the investments I made with the team of investors, a year prior, was turning south. The investors were barely fulfilling their commitment to this investment. Through it all, I was trusting God as I only moved forward with this opportunity, BY FAITH. Confident that I was obeying the Holy Spirit, therefore, God would protect me through whatever may come against me.

I was back in Tulsa for months and still traveling with the ministry. With no real movement on anything else in my life, I decided to pick back up my searching and pursue my engineering job but this time in Tulsa. Thankfully, I kept a line of communication open with my co-workers at the company I left. But was this God's will for me to return to that place? At this point, I had no idea. I just continued to pray. As you can imagine, the money I had made from the book tour was being used up on my monthly bills—mainly gasoline, cell phone, and car insurance. I watched my bank account dwindle to amounts I had not seen since my high school and college days. It had been over a year since I left my job and God has brought me this far, and according to His word, He would not leave me here. All the pride that was once in my life is now loooong gone!

Although I read the Word and knew (in my mind) that my gracious Father God would supply all of my needs according to His riches in glory by Christ Jesus (Philippians 4:19 KJV) there comes a time when all the Word that you have read becomes your reality. There were times in the month when I knew I would be short the money to pay my cell phone bill after the other bills were paid. Did I panic? Did I call for help? Yes! But not to another human. I called out to God for help!

Several thoughts were floating around in my head: 1. When will this "walking on water" or "wilderness" season be over? 2. I am trusting God to provide and make a way out of no way because I believe I obeyed Him by leaving my job. I have NEVER been in this season in my life, but I did what I am accustomed to do—pray and seek God's face! I literally shut myself in my room and prayed and soaked in God's presence. During this time, I received wisdom to call my cell phone provider to get an extension on my payment. As the grace period was ending and in the 11th hour God showed up and paid my cell phone bill for the month! Without my knowledge or asking anyone —the Holy Spirit spoke to one of God's children and had that person pay the amount. I could not do anything but give God all the praise and glory and honor! I cried my little eyes out. I was overwhelmed with God's love and mercy. At that moment, the Word of God manifested into my reality. No more, will God really provide—yes, no, maybe so. I am confident that God will perform His word. Just stand on His Word and watch Him move on your behalf. As I continued to grow spiritually in my faith and trust in the Lord, He began to reveal to me the intimate access I have to Him being His daughter. In the Bible, God uses the relationship a person has with their natural father compared to their relationship with Him, their Heavenly Father. Jesus states in Matthew 7:11, "you parents—if your children ask for a loaf of bread, do you give them a stone instead? Or if they ask for a fish, do you give them a snake? Of course not! So if you sinful people know how to give good gifts to your children, how much more will your Heavenly Father give good gifts to those who ask him?" Around this time my relationship with my natural father began to increase. Being in need and being one of his daughters, my natural father began to show me the level of access I already had to him and his resources. The level of extra care and sensitivity that my natural father began to show me when I needed it the most was amazing. But then the Holy Spirit began to reveal to me that if my natural father was doing this, how much more was He doing and will do in my time of need? The Lord is close to the brokenhearted (Psalms 34) and He was showing me just that. I indeed felt and saw the love of God move in my life. God is a good Father!

As a few more months went by, I had almost given up again my search for my engineering job that the Lord had promised when suddenly it was time! I had just arrived home from Monday night prayer at church when I decided to check my email. It was nearing 8pm and I noticed an email from a recruiter inquiring about my interest in a Manufacturing Engineering contract position in town! You would think I would be excited, but I was highly suspect. Who was this recruiter? What was the name of the company they were recruiting for? With hesitation, I replied to the recruiter's email with my many questions. And to my surprise, she responded right back with the answers to my questions. I forwarded her my resume that night and then she called me! Who does that? She was a very energetic woman and excited for me (already) about this position. She mentioned that she would forward my information on to the company and the hiring manager, but I should know that they are wanting to move pretty quickly with filling this position. It was a six-month contract position and the company was hiring four engineers to work on this huge project. Is this really happening? Could this be it? Is this the position the Holy Spirit told me about regarding returning to engineering? Let's see! This all happened on a Monday, by Friday of that same week I had my face to face interview with the hiring manager at the company. And by Monday of the following week, I was officially one of the four Manufacturing Engineers that this company hired on as a contractor! Praise THE Lord! My first day on the job was November 7th! I was nervous yet excited at the same time. It was a year and several months since I left my Manufacturing position at the company that the Holy Spirit instructed me to leave. Back at work! Wow! Money, yay!

On my first day at work, I noticed a familiar face. It was a co-worker from the company I had left. What a God move! I became work friends with this individual at my last job, so I was excited to see and know someone at this new job. Things were going great in this new position. God was really turning things around in my life just as He said He would. After a short few months, I was approached about my interest in a full-time manager position at the company but in another department other than engineering. I was super excited and began thanking God for the favor. But I quickly remembered God's promise to me regarding an engineering position. Yes, I was currently working in an engineering position, but this position was for only a 6-month term. Now I was not concerned about the 6th month because I believed I would be full time by then. I expressed my interest in the full-time position and the company's expectation was that I started in this position as soon as possible. A few weeks went by and no movement. I finally received word that the transition into this position would not be until several months from now, in May. The month of May would actually be my 6th month with the company in this contract position. Perfect. I had no worries, only peace. During this waiting time, I received surprising news from my manager. He informed the group (the three engineers and myself) that he recently took another position with another company and was moving to another state! What?! I certainly did not see this coming. Lord, what are you up to? After this sudden announcement, my manager scheduled a meeting with each person on the team. I was the first one selected to have this meeting. I had no idea what this meeting was about, but I was going in confident because I believe God was ordering my steps. Surprised yet again, my manager asked my interest in taking his full-time role! Well, of course I am interested. We chatted a little longer then the meeting was over. I returned to work as if nothing had happened. During that same week, my manager had the same meeting with the rest of the team. Guess who they extended an offer to for my manager's position?! Yep, me! I was officially back in my engineering position, full time, benefits – the works. Praise God! These were really exciting times! Total restoration at its finest…but wait it gets better!

I began training with my manager to learn everything he did before his last day at the office. During one of our training sessions in his office, he revealed some things to me: 1. My manager planned to leave the company before the summer. 2. my manager and our plant manager knew that whomever they hired for the contract positions, they would pull from this group of four to select my manager's replacement. 3. From day one they were "watching" me because they believed I would do a great job in his role. Wow…that is nobody but God! Months before the recruiter contacted me about the contract position I would often say to the people around me—I am curious to see what God is working on behind the scenes. And NOW I see! I am glad I chose to trust God with this job search and for the manifestation of the position at the right time and the right place. Just going along my day, God delivered me a package with my name on it postdated for that Monday when I received the email from the recruiter. Oh, how awesome is that? I hope this encourages you as you read. No matter what you are going through God knows the end from the beginning and the dates have already been set. I wish I had a clearer understanding of this before I started applying for those other engineering positions. We live and we learn!

Today is my manager's last day at the office, and he decided to schedule a meeting with the entire team to say his goodbyes and to inform them that I will be their new manager! I am fully aware that this could be a potentially awkward situation—me managing a group of three people that I started the company with under contract, however, I chose to be and stay positive about everything. During this meeting, while my manager was talking, I noticed a message notification on my phone. Trying to appear as if I was paying attention to my manager's speech, I was reading this message in total disbelief. The company that I quit was reaching out to me to see my interest in taking my old position back!?!?!? WHAAAAT! OMG! YESSSSS! Praise God! Wanting to burst into tears of joy, but I quickly came back to reality as I heard my manager's voice still talking to the team. Oh no, I had already signed my offer letter for this new position! Would it be wrong if I backed out at the last minute? I have never been in this situation before. What do I do? I went to lunch! I prayed and cried out to my Heavenly Father thanking Him for this amazing journey and from the looks of it bringing me full circle! Not saying a word to my current employer, I contacted my previous employer and expressed my high interest in returning and looked forward to whatever that process looked like for me. Yay! As I communicated this exciting news to my close friends, none of them gave me the response I thought this breakthrough warranted. What is the deal? Each one of them asked me if I had prayed about taking my old position back with this company. No, but I KNOW this is God! Right? Surely? So, I began to pray and ask God whether I should go back to the company that He instructed me to quit. After taking three days to fast and pray regarding this opportunity, my answer was revealed on the last day. Although my manager had already left the company, I never moved into his office. I just did not feel it necessary when I did not think I would stay. But on the last day of the fast, I had a feeling to walk over to my manager's office. So that is what I did. I walked into the office and looked on the desk and saw a notebook with a note on the front of it addressed to me from my manager. With the office lights still off, I grabbed the notebook and walked out. The note was a thank you for doing a good job so far and that he believed that I would do a great job in his position. This may seem small, but I believed this note was my confirmation to stay put at my current employer. Really Lord?! I have "sacrificed" working for my previous employer twice! But I trust God and BY FAITH I contacted my previous employer with a thank you for the opportunity, but I will stay put at my current employer. This was almost as hard as leaving the company the first time! I was a little sad, but my attitude changed because I believe this is God's perfect will for my life. You cannot get more perfect than God's perfect!

After this confirmation, I moved over to MY office and was getting settled in nicely. I was actually getting excited about this new opportunity when the shift happened! One day, I was asked by a coworker my interest in attending an upcoming training course. I agreed and received my manager's approval. The course time arrived and we were away from the office for four days. On the last day of the class, I received a phone call from one of the guys on my team. I missed the call due to being in class but sent a text to him in response to his call. He immediately called me back. Then I knew something must have happened. So I walked out of class to answer his call by which at the same time my coworker received a call and was walking out of class. My phone call went something like this, "Hello?" "Hey Meagan, I'm sorry to tell you this, but our office was just closed." (Laughing) "What do you mean?" "I am serious Meagan, our office was just closed and everyone was laid off!" (Confused) "Wow, okay, thanks for telling me." "Ok, I am leaving the office now because they are making everyone leave." "Okay, take care." Looking over to my hysterical coworker who just finished his phone call as well, I asked if he heard. He said, "Yeah, we have to go back to the office." I said okay. I quickly packed my things up in the classroom and headed for my car, praying along the way. I decided to call the HR personnel to confirm and get further instructions. He confirmed the layoff and asked for my return back to the office. On my drive back, many thoughts came to my mind—one being I need to contact my previous employer to see if that position is still open! My second thought was, did I miss God about staying put and not taking the other position? My third thought was this is not the final verdict for me. No ma'am and no sir! I had crazy peace and I knew my God was working on something! I asked the Holy Spirit for instructions and guidance. Instructions and guidance was given. I needed to know what to do. I was led to contact my coworker at my current employer (who was also my coworker at my previous employer) to see what had happened! We spoke on the phone, and she confirmed that things were crazy at the office but before we finished our conversation she said something that confirmed my next steps. She is still friends with coworkers from our previous company and had heard about the position that was open (the same position they contacted me about) and suggested that I contact our previous employer about this position that day! Wow! I know this is surely God because I had not mentioned my communication with my previous employer with anyone. That is confirmation! So I texted my contact at my previous employer and updated them on the current situation. I inquired about the position whether it was still open. A few minutes had passed and the response I got truly blessed my soul! I prayed and said, "Lord I believe what is for me is for me." It had been almost 2-3 weeks since this position was open. My contact person responded back and that a candidate had not been selected and interviews were still in process. They prompted me to apply online for the position right away! Hallelujah! I obeyed and applied online. The following day, the recruiter for that position conducted my phone interview and scheduled my face to face interview the following week! I got the job! Total restoration! Same company, same office, close to the same salary, and in the same position that I had quit! Only My God could orchestrate this!

When God promised me restoration, I took hold of His promise! I was also believing for restoration regarding this investment opportunity I embarked on. What started out as an exciting new way to serve God turned into a total scam! After two years of being one of many investors with this team of investor, it was brought to our attention that this investor team was running a Ponzi scheme on innocent people around the United States! This is horrible, especially, for this team of investors to be using the name of the Lord to attract potential investors. Because of this scheme, many of the investors, including myself, were forced to file for bankruptcy. I tell you, I have experienced so many things during this short time that I never saw coming but through it all, I can confidently say all is well. Even through this difficult time with the investor team, hatred nor bitterness never crept into my heart. Why? Because my motives were to obey God and nothing else. He honored that and protected me and developed my character. The Word of God says in Romans 5:3-5, "We can rejoice, too, when we run into problems and trials, for we know that they help us develop endurance. And endurance develops strength of character, and character strengthens our confident hope of salvation. And this hope will not lead to disappointment. For we know how dearly God loves us because he has given us the Holy Spirit to fill our hearts with his love." I can honestly say that this situation has not tainted my view of people, investments nor God Himself. I often question within myself if I missed the leading of the Holy Spirit regarding this. I do not know. Of course, I did not want to go through this but look at all the things I have learned that I would not have learned otherwise. It is all about perspective. Yes, I am human. The spirit of fear and definitely shame has come to hinder my forward movement in the things of God but I declare that NO weapon formed against me shall prosper. I know my God is fighting for me because of the peace I have and the fact that I consistently see His hand moving in my life.

Once I was restored back to my job, the Holy Spirit instructed me to get my own place again. YEEESSS! But I had sowed or sold all my things, and I was going through bankruptcy! You think this is too big for God? Ha! Around this time, I was inquiring about homes/apartments/condos for rent in the city. I was quickly connected to a business owner that was looking for someone to rent their two-bedroom condo, semi furnished and within my budget! Also, they do not require credit checks for renting! Now you can shout! My God is good and He is extremely faithful to those that trust Him and follow His ways! Praise God! Some may say, "Meagan that was too much!" I would passionately say to those individuals, "but do you not see God's hand in all of this?" BY FAITH I quit my job, followed Jesus and experienced God like never before. Once this assignment was complete, God Himself totally restored me! This is only the beginning! I believe that God tests His children quite often so see where our hearts lie and our trust resides. It is extremely easy to say—I trust God—but our actions really determine the validity of this statement. God calls us the "light of the world" in Matthew 5:14, so let your lives shine for Jesus in this dark and broken world. I pray that my testimony has encouraged you to live boldly for Jesus. Not in a way that is crazy and reckless in "Jesus' Name" but BY FAITH obeying the Holy Spirit's instructions for your life. God will not lead you astray.

"May the Lord bless you and protect you. May the Lord smile on you and be gracious to you. May the Lord show you his favor and give you his peace." Numbers 6:24-26

PRINCIPLES TO LIVE BY

PRINCIPLE 1: Read Your Bible Daily

PRINCIPLE 2: Pray Daily

PRINCIPLE 3: Have Fun

PRINCIPLE 4: Embrace the Journey

PRINCIPLE 1: *Read Your Bible Daily*

Some of us have good memories, and some of us have selective memory but getting in the habit of reading your Bible daily will help you to remember the ways of the Lord. Several times in the Bible, God instructed His leaders to read and meditate on His Word daily. This helps us connect better with our Heavenly Father and to become more intimate with Him.

PRINCIPLE 2: *Pray Daily*

Praying is simply communication with God our Father. As you develop a relationship with Him, like all of our other relationships, communication is important for the sustainability of that relationship. It can start first thing in the morning by saying, Good morning Holy Spirit. That was not too bad, was it? As you develop your intimacy (closeness) with God, your prayers will come out naturally.

PRINCIPLE 3: *Have Fun*

God is not a boring God, and surely our walk with Him should not be boring either. As a King's kid, we must remember that our standards for living do not come from this world but from our Father who is in Heaven. Enjoy Kingdom living and the abundant life!

PRINCIPLE 4: *Embrace the Journey*

Although walking BY FAITH is not comfortable embrace your own unique journey with the Holy Spirit. Saying yes to live for Jesus will take you places your mind had not even considered! Let God use your life for His glory for the world to see.

PUBLISHED MATERIAL BY MEAGAN PINKNEY

Waiting While You Wait: My Journey Through Singleness

In this book, I will share several personal testimonies from my journey as a single woman as I have learned to wait on God. When an individual yields them self to the Holy Spirit, for the use of the Kingdom, you will be amazed by the testimonies you will be able to share. Instead of me forgetting all the wonderful, supernatural things God has done in and through my life, I wanted to write all of them down to pass on to other Believers, especially those who are currently single. I believe it is an extremely important task to pass on to others what God can and will do for us if we learn to wait on Him (like a waiter) while we are in the process of waiting (for the purpose)! The purpose of this book is to motivate individuals to lean on God for everything, whether big or small. God loves us dearly and He wants to see us prosper. Singles should know that singleness is a beautiful thing and should definitely be valued as it is a blessing from God- whether you are single for a season or a lifetime.

Pray Eat Lift: My Journey Through Weightloss

In today's society, everyone wants to know how to lose weight instantly. Some recommendations are to explore those celebrity and military diets or just simply not eating. To be honest, if this could be done everyone would do it…right? Being conscious of our weight or waistline is something that a majority of people can relate to. According to the Centers for Disease Control and Prevention (CDC), more than one-third (34.9% or 78.6 million) of U.S. adults are obese. I can only speak for myself that I do not want to be included in that 34.9%, but in reality I was stuck there for several years of my young life until something changed! In this book, I will share my personal testimony of my supernatural weight loss journey. My journey, although quite unique, will encourage you and hopefully kick-start your own personal weight loss journey and relationship with the Holy Spirit. Whether we realize it or not the excess weight that we are physically carrying around is a huge hindrance to our productiveness in life. Once we can develop a healthy balance of praying, eating and lifting then our journey can begin.

Inner Circle: One God Three Friends

This book will display the journey of one God and three women earnestly seeking God's perfect will in their lives. With the leading of the Holy Spirit, we stepped out to trust God's ultimate desire for Kingdom relationships. Through our journey of discovery, you will be encouraged along your walk to know that you too can experience divine connections, find accountability, friendship, purpose and so much more. Come along with us on this journey. (Meagan Pinkney is a contributing author)

Daily Dose of Declarations

A 365 Day Journey To Help You Declare Positive Affirmations Over Your Life. (Meagan Pinkney is a contributing author)

To book Meagan Pinkney or to purchase products and packages please contact her at:

www.meaganpinkney.com

(539) 302-3848

www.ingramcontent.com/pod-product-compliance
Lightning Source LLC
Chambersburg PA
CBHW050444010526
44118CB00013B/1670